12

Simple

Steps

To

Better Sales

Shark Bite Coaching

ISBN: 0615846696
ISBN-13: 978-0615846699

Discover Basic Techniques that will Help You Substantially Boost Your Sales & Increase Your Revenue

DEDICATION

This book is dedicated to entrepreneurs and business professionals who are ready to take their businesses to the next level.

I wish you luck in your success and hope that I can help even just a little bit.

CONTENTS

INTRODUCTION

Originally written and administered as an e-course, each chapter of 12 Simple Steps to Better Sales will teach you valuable information on how you can successfully boost your sales and increase your revenue.

Reading old books and magazines on how to be a better salesperson or entrepreneur will give you little or no help at all, simply because today's businesses work at a pace and style that the world has never seen before. This book doesn't just provide you with important information, but we have made sure that all the tips, keys, and lessons here are all up-to-date and trending with current events, especially with the Internet and all that entails!

Although we provide just 12 key chapters in this guide, rest assured that we won't leave you hanging, as we will also give you ideas and advice on how to use these Simple Steps to get the best possible results.

All the information presented here is given in a clear manner for ease of understanding and a quick read. [The sooner you get through the book, the faster you can start increasing your sales, right?] So what are you waiting for? Turn to the next page and learn the best, simplest steps to quickly increase your sales and easily grow your business!

CHAPTER ONE – THE BASICS

Here are just a few basic tips that can help you start increasing your sales as soon as possible.

In today's economy, many small businesses and entrepreneurs are looking for simple and effective ways to increase sales, but with consumers spending less and profit margins getting smaller they are finding that they have less money to spend on advertising and marketing. This is causing business owners and professionals to work harder and many are looking for more creative, cost effective ways to generate leads and, ultimately, sales.

This isn't necessarily a bad thing as many small businesses and privately-owned companies are doing better in today's marketplace than their larger counterparts, simply because they're becoming more innovative with their sales processes.

Here are a few quick tips to help you increase sales for your business. While you may be familiar with some of these methods already, they are all solid and effective techniques that you can implement immediately.

Always qualify your prospects

When your budget is tight and your time is important it's necessary for you to make sure that your efforts are going to achieve results. When it comes to determining potential customers, the faster you can validate prospects, the better. A great way to start this is to document certain customer traits that would indicate a qualified prospect such as having a specific problem which your product can solve. Another might be if their goals can be accomplished using your product. Lastly, you determine if their "pain" can be relieved by your product.

Do your best to gain trust

While **price** and **product benefits** are obvious buying factors, the less obvious ones are **intuition**, **impressions**, and **rapport**. It's important to keep in mind that people are just as likely to buy for emotional reasons as for practical ones, so do your best to show them that you're sincere, and that you honor your business arrangements. In other words, never make a promise to a new prospect that you don't intend to keep. In fact, it's always best to underpromise and overdeliver than the other way around.

Define your unique selling proposition

If your product or service provides your customer with specific benefits, do your best to make sure that they are unique and differentiate you from your competition. Make sure you express clearly how that unique feature will benefit the client and adds value to your offering. A client is more likely to be interested in what's in it for them. Make sure your unique selling proposition is completely detailed using the "FAB" approach—Feature, Advantage, Benefit. Keep in mind that this will only impress the client if the "Benefit" is specifically focused on his/her "pain."

Listen to your customer

When it comes to selling, most people are guilty of "overselling" and end up losing out on the sale. It's important to listen to your prospect as they ask questions and respond to your queries. Be aware of tone, and pay close attention to body language. If you take the time to listen to your customer, you may be able to uncover their real problem, provide them with a unique solution, and successfully close the sale.

Make your presentation sparkle

Never take your sales presentation for granted. Before meeting with a potential client, make sure you practice your pitch. After all, you've spent a lot of money and time perfecting your product or service, so why not take the time to develop a polished and effective presentation? A poorly carried out presentation is one of the fastest ways to lose a sale. You must be confident in what you're presenting. Start with all the important details and benefits first since you wouldn't want your client to be baffled by an abrupt overload of information. Structure your information following the FAB formula and it may prompt a deeper conversation with your potential customer. The more open dialogue you have, the greater the chance of closing the sale.

Do your homework

Before any meeting, always take time to research your prospect so that you can show that you have a solid understanding of their business needs, ask more informed questions to get more in-depth answers, and be well-prepared and confident before your meeting.

Without selling your products or services, there will be no revenue for your business, so with every new prospect you must create a positive, engaging experience. Remember, happy, satisfied customers will buy more products and will often refer other customers to you!

CHAPTER TWO – SETTING REALISTIC GOALS

In the last chapter we talked about basic, yet effective ways to increase sales right away. Now we are going to talk about setting realistic sales goals for yourself and your business.

Oh, that wonderful feeling when we close a sale! There's nothing like it! It fills us with a sense of accomplishment and achievement, which in turn motivates us to sell even more.

If you've ever been in a situation where you have been given unobtainable goals from a supervisor or sales managers, then you know there is nothing worse than being unable to achieve your goals or make your quota. The results are the same, whether you work for someone else or you work for yourself. You're left with a feeling of despair that leads to a lack of morale and even lower sales figures across the board.

FACT: Unrealistic goals will result in fewer sales and lower revenue.

It's important to keep in mind that when you're setting your sales goals for the year, don't set your expectations too high. Although you want to achieve maximum results, being realistic is the key to your overall success.

A technique in establishing realistic goals is through setting long-term and short-term goals. A long-term goal is important as it enables you to focus on it and channel your energy to it. It helps you to stay on the right track. Short-term objectives are equally important since they allow you to achieve your long-term goals in smaller steps, and you can check on your progress regularly.

You want to put a plan in place that allows you to reach your projected goals and current objectives at a steady pace without putting unnecessary stress on yourself or your sales team. This is important simply because success itself is a great motivator. If you start out with small, obtainable goals you will find that you and your team will be more motivated to reach higher. On the other hand, if you set unrealistic or unattainable goals, the opposite will occur as morale dwindles.

Here is a simple but SMART formula for setting realistic and attainable sales goals. This formula is referred to as SMART because it stands for:

Specific

Measurable

Attainable

Realistic

Timely

This simple yet catchy sales acronym has been around for many years and has helped many companies and business owners to develop effective sales plans that are realistic enough to be achieved in a timely manner.

- **S**pecific means you set goals that are well-defined and focused.

- **M**easurable indicates the need for criteria to measure progress.

- **A**ttainable goals are those that you can actually meet or exceed; they are not over-the-top or too challenging.

- **R**ealistic indicates the importance of choosing goals that matter.

- **T**imely means you must set a time frame for achieving these goals. Open-ended goals are the ones that are never achieved.

It's important to be specific when it comes to what you want to accomplish. When it comes to setting realistic goals, the key to making it work is taking your time with each step and maintaining relevance in your daily activities to move you closer to achieving your objectives, and ultimately, your goals. Don't forget to include a solid plan for putting them into action along with criteria to evaluate the effectiveness of your actions on your sales numbers.

CHAPTER THREE – BUILD RAPPORT

Now that you know how to set realistic sales goals, it's time to learn about how to get your customers to relax and feel comfortable enough to close the sale.

Getting your customer to relax is important for any type of sales situation. It's a good idea to think of the customer as a guest in your home, where, as host, you want to make them as comfortable as possible. The more comfortable they are, the easier it will be for them to talk to you and to open up about real in-depth issues he/she is facing.

If you've been in sales for any length of time I'm sure you are well aware that trying to persuade someone you've never met before to buy your product or service is extremely challenging, if not impossible, to say the least.

While the challenges are many, the main reason for failure is most consumers have a general and basic fear—and predetermined stereotype— associated with sales people. The fear that they are all alike puts all sales and business development professionals in the same category as a used car salesman. They are afraid of being convinced to buy something they don't need at a price they can't afford.

When it comes to acquiring a new customer and closing the sale, an off topic conversation is a great icebreaker. While we all want to make that initial sale right away, the ultimate goal should be to obtain a lifetime customer—creating the opportunity for repeat sales. So take a little time to get to know your customer better. Try to find a common denominator that you can both relate to, something unrelated to their problem and the solution you are trying to sell them.

This is easier than you may think; people love to talk, especially about themselves. Ask questions about their families, their pets, and their hobbies. Be likeable. Make them feel that you are a great person who loves to listen.

A false misconception related to dealing with people is that charm can close a sale. Well, charm alone cannot close sales. Rather, this is important if you want your customers to be comfortable with you. Charisma helps you in building rapport.

When it comes to attracting new customers it's important to always be prepared. You never know where you might obtain a new customer. Did you know that most customer acquisition happens outside of the workplace? Not only at business and networking functions, but you may also find prospects at your local grocery store, at sporting events, and restaurants.

Here is a quick example. Say you're in the pet food aisle at your local grocery store. This is a good place to talk to people, because people love to talk about their pets. A simple question such as "What kind of dog do you have?" will get them talking. Just make sure they were picking up dog food and not bird seed—it helps to be observant.

The junk food aisles [chips/candy/soda] are also a good place to talk to people. For some reason, the presence of candy and junk food puts people in a good mood, and they are more likely to join in a conversation with a stranger. This can open the door to future communication and may eventually lead to acquiring them as a customer.

Now, I'm not saying that you should start stalking the aisles of your favorite super market [probably not against the law, but it's pretty weird]. I'm just saying that you should always be prepared, because you never know where an opportunity may present itself. The simple fact is that most people love to talk as long as they can relate to the main topic of conversation, so don't be afraid to ask questions, and get to know your customer beyond what they may need from you.

The more comfortable you can make your customer, the better off you both will be, and the more sales you will make.

CHAPTER FOUR – FILL THE FUNNEL

Now that you know how important it is to make your customer comfortable, we are going to chat about following up with a lead before it cools off.

Anyone that works in sales knows just how important it is to have lead sources to keep their sales funnel full. But it's not just about how we obtain the leads that is important, it's what we do with them once we have them in hand.

In sales terms, the longer a lead goes without receiving a response or contact of some kind, the colder it becomes. Failing to follow up with a lead immediately after it's received is one of the biggest mistakes that anyone in the sales profession can make.

There are many reasons why a lead will go cold. For instance: they could have gone someplace else to find the solution they needed. Or they could have been contacted by another business or purchased from a competitor who wasn't slow about following up on a lead. Or they could have changed their mind completely. You may consider it a single loss but that lead could have entailed additional sales, referrals, and more potential customers.

When it comes to making sales, it doesn't particularly matter what you're selling, but it is extremely important that you get to know who you are selling what to. That is why it is vital that you follow-up with any new lead as soon as possible. Remember, as we discussed in the previous chapter you want to make your 'new' potential customer feel relaxed and at ease from the very start, and not getting back to them quickly will no doubt get you started off on the wrong foot.

That old adage "strike while the iron is hot" still holds true. In fact, the faster you can respond to a new customer, the better. It is important that you make contact with them and start building a relationship while they are still interested in what you have to offer.

Another common mistake is having absolutely no enthusiasm once you contact them. When you call a potential customer, stand up and smile as you speak to them; the customer will pick up on the inflection in your voice and respond to it in kind. Don't act as though they are an inconvenience or burden to you. Make time for them and remember to treat them just like they are a new friend you are excited to be speaking with.

Remember, you are the expert when it comes to your product, so don't expect your customer to know everything; if they did, they wouldn't need you. And always make sure they know that you are happy to help them.

Another no-no when following up on a lead is to yawn, sneeze, or cough into the receiver of the phone. I understand that these are normal and common bodily functions, but there is no excuse for doing it directly into the receiver. It looks like you don't care how your potential customer sees you; these are great ways to lose a sale and lose a potential customer forever. The yawn alone will most likely make the customer hang up the phone.

Always put yourself in the shoes of the customer. Imagine meeting someone for the first time over the telephone, and your conversation is being interrupted by yawns and sneezes, and I doubt you would be gung-ho about doing business with them.

Following up with a lead and then putting them on hold is another common mistake. Although your reasons for putting them on hold may seem very important to you, your lead will find it annoying regardless of your reasons. So be sure to set aside a time to follow up with your new lead when you know there is enough time to speak without interruption.

And in today's age of technological reliance, sending an email is simple—but not enough. Utilize email as a way to initiate a follow-up and perhaps attach some information you know they may be interested in or that they have requested. Then follow up with a phone call to humanize the relationship. It is still essential to create a personal bond, not just a virtual one.

Keep in mind that the next time you receive a lead, act on it immediately, let your customers know that you are happy to work with them, speak clearly and avoid interruptions, and watch your sales productivity increase!

CHAPTER FIVE – HAPPY CUSTOMERS BEGETS MORE CUSTOMERS

Now we are moving on to using testimonials to make more sales.

If you've ever made a purchase from QVC, HSN, or watched an infomercial on TV [anyone who has ever had trouble sleeping has definitely been exposed to infomercials...], then I'm sure you're aware of the power of testimonials. You see, they know the secret. They know that by harnessing the power of customer testimony they can increase their sales substantially without spending additional funds on advertising.

Reading or seeing the testimonies of others can help potential customers imagine what it would be like to own the product themselves or take advantage of the service that you offer. When a person goes shopping for a particular product or service, one of the first things they take into consideration is the opinion of others.

They will take the advice of family, friends, strangers and even reviews on websites. They do this because they want to make an informed choice. The comments help them picture what it would be like to experience the same benefits as the person who shared his testimony with them.

One of the best ways to get perspective new customers to purchase from you is to introduce them to other satisfied customers, and since you can't take your current (happy) customers to every business meeting or sales call you go on, it is important to collect these reviews and testimonials to share with new prospects.

While this is a fairly easy step to take, many business professionals take it for granted, and the cold hard facts are that they are just leaving money on the table!

The process is simple! All you have to do is ask your best customers if you can interview them about the positive experience they've had with your product or service. You either take their written testimonial, or if they'll allow it, record it with an audio recorder or even a digital camera. Be sure to inform them how you're going to use the information so they will be at ease knowing that you're going to be using their words and images in front of perspective customers.

Once you have several testimonials, you can present them in printed or digital format. Creating a digital presentation is as easy as plugging your customer's audio or video testimony into a PowerPoint presentation that you can playback on your laptop for prospective customers.

Ask your best customers to talk about the benefits they receive from using your product or service. Try to collect several different testimonials relating to different aspects of your business, products or services. This way you can use the one that best fits the new customer you are working with.

Another good tip is to show pictures of customers using your product or service. Combine a glowing testimonial with a picture of a happy satisfied customer and it will be worth more than a thousand high color brochures, not to mention a lot less expensive!

Remember, nothing sells better than truth and you can't get closer to the truth than when it comes from someone who's had a real life experience with you, your product, your services, and your company.

While you are gathering testimonials, why not also ask your satisfied customers if they would be a live reference for you. Be sure to find out how they would prefer to be contacted by your potential customers before giving out their information.

CHAPTER SIX – NEW LEADS ARE LEADS NOW

In the last chapter we discussed how to use testimonials to make more sales. In this chapter we cover the importance of taking full advantage of every new lead that you receive.

As we have discussed before, every day in business is critical and every potential sale is important. Remember that the lead you receive today could very well be in the hands of your competition tomorrow. With that in mind, I can't stress enough the importance of capitalizing on your leads as soon as you receive them.

New leads are not meant to be pinned to a bulletin board or written on a sticky note and just posted on your computer monitor. They are meant to be acted on as soon as possible.

When it comes to the thought processes of any consumer, their first instinct is to shop around for a new product or service by researching on the Internet, making phone calls and asking questions. So with any new lead that you receive, you can safely assume that they have also looked at or checked with at least one of your competitors (probably more).

The timing on a lead is so important. The moment you receive the lead, pick up the phone and make contact with that person. If you wait too long, two things could happen:

Your competition will get the jump on you.

OR

You will be giving your potential customer time to find another solution to their problem.

By letting a hot lead sit around and cool off, you are almost guaranteed to lose that sale. Put yourself in the shoes of the consumer. Would you appreciate receiving a call several days after your initial inquiry? Not at all, and I'm pretty sure that by then you would've lost interest and moved on to another option for fulfilling your needs.

I don't think your customer would appreciate a phone call a week after you have received their information. Even if they are still on the market for your product, you won't be off to a good start.

Now let's go over a few other common mistakes that are often made when it comes to following up with a new lead.

Giving up on a lead too soon.

It's sad but true that many business professionals give up on a new lead too soon, eliminating any possibility of closing the sale. It is important to have a system in place for continuous follow-up. You need to create a plan for contacting a new lead multiple times before you move them to the dead pile. Only you can decide how many times that will be, but the standard contact scenario is 7 to 8 times before closing a sale.

Let's take this point by the numbers. Here are the statistics of when average sales professionals usually give up on a lead.

- 48% quit after the 1st call
- 24% quit after the 2nd call
- 12% quit after the 3rd call
- 6% quit after the 4th call
- 10% quit after the 5th call onwards

Almost half of sales professionals would give up on the first contact but there is a very good reason not to give up on a lead too soon! Below are the figures of when an average sale closes:

- 2% close on the 1st call
- 3% close on the 2nd call
- 4% close on the 3rd call
- 10% close on the 4th call
- 81% close on the 5th call onwards

These figures indicate that a deal is closed on the 5th contact and onwards. Persistence is a must when it comes to sales. Giving up too soon is like throwing away money and new customers.

Assuming that your new lead is ready to buy on first contact.

This goes back to relationship building. As we have discussed before it is important to find common ground with your new potential customer. While this may take some time it is an important part of the process, so that you can build a level of trust between you and your potential customer. Despite the fact figures say latter contacts are when deals usually close, one should aim to make the best impression on the first contact and build your relationship on a strong foundation from there. The initial impression you make can affect your relationship with your client later on.

Just remember to always keep in mind that leads are meant to be acted on, so the next time you receive a hot lead, don't waste any time making that initial contact.

"Strike while the Iron's Hot"

CHAPTER SEVEN – TRIED AND TRUE

For chapter seven we are going to go over a few tried (not tired) and true methods that you can use to increase your sales.

When it comes to increasing sales and income, there are many strategies that you can employ. As a matter of fact, if you do an online search for the term "increase sales," you will be barraged with hundreds and thousands of results filled with tips and advice to help you reach your goals. While we're not going to be able to cover all of those topics in this issue, we are going to go over a few tried and true methods that I like to use myself.

Even though these are simple, they are extremely effective, and when used properly can definitely help you increase your sales.

Enhance your customer's buying experience.

One of the first things we're going to talk about is making the consumers buying experience as easy as possible. While there is a lot of information that you may want to collect from your new customer, it is important not to ask for too much information up front.

Instead, ask for the bare minimum from a customer so they can complete their purchase as quickly as possible. If you want to gather more demographics from them later on, you can follow-up by sending a thank you note, asking them to fill out warranty information or take a quick customer survey.

I know this may not seem like a big deal to you but you may be surprised to find out how many sales you are losing because your checkout process is too complicated.

So, don't make your customer jump through hoops to buy your products. They'll only get frustrated and put it off until later, and most of the time, later never comes!

Stress the benefits.

When it comes to closing the sale, it's important that you talk about the benefits of your product or service and save the features for later. Your customers don't want to know ALL the details on how your product or service works right away; they first want to know how it will benefit them! Don't forget the FAB Approach (Feature, Advantage, Benefit)

Benefits show off the value of your product much better than features. Let your prospective customer know exactly what your product can do for them. Will it help them make more money, have more time, reduce their stress, give them energy, help them live longer, etc. This is what they want to know and this is what will help you sell more of your products and services. On the contrary, if you bombard them with too much information, like starting off with the history of your product or service, you are likely to bore your client or worse; you'll lose their patience and interest.

Practice good, honest communication.

As we have discussed before, communication is key. It is important to follow-up with potential buyers in a timely manner. By keeping the lines of communication open you gain more trust and credibility. This will turn into more sales for your product or service!

Encourage your customers to ask questions.

Always do your best to put them at ease and let them know that they're not bothering you or wasting your time. Answer each question honestly and promptly. Remember, customers can tell when you're lying. If you don't know the answer to the question, don't lie to them or try to make something up; just tell them you'll find out for them as soon as possible, and let them know when you do. This additional follow-up is another opportunity to build your relationship and move closer to the sale.

Another reason why honesty or transparency is essential in communicating with your client is to help avoid miscommunication later on. Convey only what your product offers and don't be too mushy by adding false or exaggerated benefits. Doing so could ruin your reputation and slam your sales.

While these are only a few simple things that you can do, they are all tried, tested, and guaranteed to be effective when it comes to increasing your sales.

CHAPTER EIGHT – AUTOMATE WITH AUTO RESPONDERS

With the previous chapter, you now know some tried and true methods that can increase your sales. In this chapter we are going to talk about using an auto responder service to help you close sales, even if you run an off-line business.

An auto responder is without a doubt one of the best marketing tools you can use. In case you aren't familiar with exactly what an auto responder is, it is a script-based application that will automatically respond to any email that it receives. Once they are triggered, they automatically start sending out a scheduled series of e-mail messages that you have carefully constructed to your prospective customers.

Auto responders are extremely fast. Once your prospect sends an e-mail requesting more information, the auto responder will deliver it almost immediately.

One of the best things about auto responders is the fact that they are always available. They are always there; ready to provide your clients and customers with the information they seek. They can free up your time so you can focus on other things. They are easy to set up and require only a small investment of your time. They can also make managing your customers and clients easier than ever because they can collect email addresses and in-depth customer demographics for you.

There's no big learning curve, so if you've never used an auto responder before, don't worry, it's really not that difficult. If your business doesn't have a website, that's not a problem either. Most auto responder services are run from their own websites if you don't have a website of your own.

You're not restricted either. You can virtually preset any auto responder to send a variety of messages. You can use them to inform your clients about future products, services, and sales. Auto responders will work for you day or night, making your company information available to anyone whenever they might request it.

As we have discussed before, not all consumers are impulse buyers. As a matter of fact, research has shown that it may take five or more contacts with the prospective customer to finally close the sale. You have the responsibility to take good care of them by feeding them valuable information. And an auto responder can help you achieve that.

While an auto responder can't do all of the work for you, it can help lighten your load immensely. It does this by sending out basic information specifically requested from the consumer that can assist with training, support, and yes, to closing more sales.

This also works very well if a customer has purchased from you before, because then you can use it to send out order confirmations, thank you notes, and even offer discounts on additional purchases, which will help increase your backend, or add on sales as well. You can always repeat your business and make money from the same mailing list whenever you have new products or services.

When it comes to choosing an auto responder for your business there are many options available. All you need to do is a quick search online and you will be amazed at all the different services to choose from. I've put together a quick list of five popular services that I have used or researched to help you narrow down your choices. While these aren't the only ones available, in my experience they all have a nice variety of features and stellar reputations.

Constant Contact: http://www.constantcontact.com

Constant Contact offers some premade email templates and gives you the ability to personalize your own from scratch.

IContact: http://www.icontact.com

They can also provide you with a marketing expert to research your competitors and industry.

Aweber: http://www.aweber.com

This system is easy to setup, powerful enough for large opt-in lists and is said to have the highest delivery rate.

Get Response: http://www.getresponse.com

Allows you to send a follow-up e-mail at specific time intervals after a client subscribes to you. It also includes an easy mailing list management system.

Mail Chimp: http://www.mailchimp.com

The service is free for the first 2,000 subscribers. It is also very user-friendly since it comes with a pre-made template wizard.

Auto responders are in a constant state of readiness so you don't have to be. So why not take some time to set up an auto responder or a series of auto responders with information that may be of interest to your customers and potential customers? I guarantee it can help your sales process run faster and smoother when incorporated into your sales routine early and often.

Need help setting up, writing or scheduling your auto responders? Email me at info@social-media-management-group.com.

CHAPTER NINE – PRODUCTS DON'T USUALLY SELL THEMSELVES

Knowing how to use an auto responder service to help increase your sales can be very helpful, so now we are going to talk about why even the best products don't sell themselves.

Just because you have the best product in the world doesn't mean that it will sell all by itself. Chances are you've heard the term "if you build it, they will come". In the world of sales that translates to "if you make it, it will sell". It's a wonderful dream, but it doesn't really work like that.

While this may have been true many decades ago, the simple truth of the matter is that there just weren't as many options back then, and chances were if you made it, it would sell, simply because of lack of competition. That doesn't hold true today, especially with the incorporation of high-speed technology that is now being used to spread consumer products on a global-scale faster than ever before.

These days, just because you have a better product doesn't mean that the product will automatically sell itself and make you rich. In the past, people weren't swamped with tons of advertising. Anything new or better stood out and was easily noticed by the masses. Today, if you have a better coffee pot, investment plan, or even a car that runs on a few drops of water, you are still fighting an uphill battle against consumer skepticism and high-budget advertising campaigns.

To sell enough of your product or service so that you can actually see a profit, you need to get the word out to the masses in a way that will catch their attention and keep it long enough to make a purchase. The days of just putting a shiny new product on the shelf and talking about how wonderfully it works are long gone. As we have discussed before, you need to convey the benefits of your new product in such a way that people will want to purchase your brand over the other 4,000 (ok, maybe I am exaggerating a little) competitors offering a slightly different version of the same thing.

It is vital that you learn how to stand out in a crowded marketplace and perfect your approach. People aren't easily sold on anything anymore, and you have to convince them that your product or service is different, better, and extraordinary. You must have a unique selling point and you must be prepared to tell them all about it.

Try the FAB method—Feature, Advantage, Benefit. Keep in mind that without a truly compelling benefit, the customer won't care about the feature or the advantage.

Do whatever it takes to 'shock and impress' your target market. Be sure to always give them something to remember. You should also be a good communicator in order to get the desired impact from a prospect.

For example: If you are in marketing, it doesn't help if you keep talking about how good your marketing company is. It doesn't matter how efficient your marketing division is or how impressive your company's background may be.

Chances are if you are with a good company, your prospect knows your company's reputation. The key questions on your prospect's mind are:

- *Why should we bring our business to you over your competitor down the street?*

- *What can you do for me that your competitors can't?*

- *What can YOU offer that will set you apart from the others?*

It's very important that you remember that people buy from YOU, not just the company and not just a product! So when you're trying to stand out in a crowded marketplace, don't just focus on the features, advantages, and benefits of your product or service and expect them to be sold on it. Focus on what your product can do for your customer, and most importantly concentrate your efforts on what YOU can personally do for them.

CHAPTER TEN – CREDIBILITY AND BRANDING

I do hope you remember the main message of chapter nine, which I'll sum up as "even the best products don't sell themselves." In this chapter we will talk about how building credibility and branding yourself can help you to enhance brand awareness and increase your sales.

Today, the average consumer is spoiled. When it comes to purchasing products, they have a wide variety of options. They have the ability to research and compare products with just a few clicks of the mouse. While you may not have the most popular product in the marketplace, you can still put yourself in a position as the 'best' by employing a few good marketing strategies.

Here are some questions you should ask yourself to aid in the development of your strategy:

Question number 1: What makes you different from your main competitor(s)?

If you're goal is to increase sales of your products and services, you have to stand out in today's crowded marketplace. Have one or more compelling benefits that differentiates you, your company, or your product/service from your competitors. Be sincere to your clients as you speak to them of the pros and cons of your product or service.

Question number 2: How will you establish yourself as an authority in your target market?

As we have discussed before, consumers are inherently skeptical when it comes to making a purchase on being "sold" on something. Because there is so much competition in today's global marketplace, it is much harder to acquire and keep new customers than ever before.

This is where branding yourself and your business as an authority comes into play. When you are recognized as an expert in your marketplace, people are much more likely to trust what you have to say and purchase the products and services that you recommend.

Branding consists of the perception consumers have of your company or product; emotions that prospects feel when they think about your company or product; and the comfort level when your target market comes to you to solve a problem. Usually prospects would engage you or your company because they believe you are credible.

Branding and building credibility virtually go hand-in-hand. While branding will help you make that first sale, credibility is what will help you keep your customers coming back for more!

FACT: When you take the time to build credibility for yourself and your business, you become a trusted brand. It will now take less time to make repeat sales from existing customers and the new customers that they refer, compared to acquiring them the first time.

It's important to understand that when it comes to branding and building credibility, you shouldn't just focus on branding your business, product or service. You also have to brand yourself. As I mentioned above, being an authority in your marketplace helps build trust, which encourages customer loyalty and almost always results in more sales. If it doesn't, perhaps you are not positioning your product correctly. Let's take a look at it together. Email shark@sharkbitecoaching.com.

Some may say that branding and credibility are not that important when it comes to closing sales, but I disagree. By taking the time to properly position yourself as an expert in front of your target audience, you are setting yourself apart from your competition in a big way.

And that's not all, when you build your own credibility, you become the 'go to' guy or gal when people think of purchasing the products or services that you offer, therefore saving you time and money when it comes to acquiring new customers or locating new prospects.

So when it comes to taking time to brand yourself and your business don't take it for granted. Building your brand and credibility is not *optional* if you truly want to succeed in increasing sales and in the long-term success of your business. It is a must to keep your business alive.

There are various ways to do this which include: social media; speaking engagements; complimentary information sessions/workshops; white papers; and industry organization participation. To discuss even more options email me at shark@sharkbitecoaching.com. I can certainly help you to take a bite and leave your mark.

CHAPTER ELEVEN – QUALIFY YOUR LEADS

In the last chapter we discussed how to build credibility and the importance of proper branding and positioning. Now we will move on to the importance of qualifying your leads.

While going out of your way to please and pamper your customers to win their loyalty and their business isn't necessarily a bad thing, it isn't always a good thing either. As a matter of fact, if you spend too much time bending over backwards just to win them over, you may be in for a huge disappointment if all of your wooing is turned down flat and results in zero sales.

As we have discussed before, consumers are smart, and they are also very savvy and wary of anyone who is trying to sell them something. But that doesn't stop them from taking full advantage of your hospitality before they tell you to hit the road. If you truly want to increase your sales and build your business, it's important that you learn how to separate the real prospective customers from the ones who are just window shopping and looking for a freebie or two.

When it comes to weeding out serious leads from the ones who will simply waste your time, it is important to have a solid process in place for prioritizing and qualifying them. You can do this by simply having a list of questions ready to weave into the conversation.

These can be as simple as asking them:

- How they found out about you
- If they were referred to you by someone else
- Whether they are experiencing problems
- If they need a solution immediately or are just shopping around
- If they have the means to purchase and are ready to buy now if the right solution presented itself

Depending on what type of business you're in or what product or service you're trying to sell, the questions may vary. The point is that the process doesn't have to be difficult and the questions don't have to be complicated. If you want to learn anything, you need to ask questions.

You will be amazed to find out how quickly you can identify the difference between a prospect that is serious and the one that is just 'kicking tires' by simply asking a few simple questions. As a matter of fact, most of the time you will be able to determine whether or not they really want your product or service within the first few minutes of your conversation.

Now what do you do if you are encountered by a window shopper? One thing I can suggest is to give them your card to contact you in the future. Who knows? They could become a qualified prospect at some point and possibly a good source of referrals in the meantime.

By taking the time to make sure that your new leads meet your established criteria for a preferred customer, you are not only saving time but you will also be sure that you are attracting high quality customers which will also have a positive impact on sales.

CHAPTER TWELVE – MOTIVATING THE BUYER

For the last chapter, we are going to talk briefly about what motivates people to buy.

Seriously, what motivates people to buy? What motivates you to buy a product?

This is the one question that everyone who has a product or service to sell wants to know the answer to. After all, if you know how to motivate your potential customers to buy, then you will be able to quickly increase your sales and your conversion rate, which is the ultimate goal of anyone in sales.

So, what is the answer to that question? What really does motivate people to buy?

It is often said that you should give people what they need,

because that is what they are going to buy. That may well have been the case a few decades ago, but sadly in today's marketplace, things have changed and people no longer buy based on what they need.

Instead, they buy what they want. This might surprise you, but statistics show that in today's media driven society, people are actually spending more money on the things that they want, such as plasma TV's, satellite systems, and recreational vehicles than they are on the necessities like food and shelter!

So it only stands to reason that if you have a product or service that you are trying to sell, you need to present it to your prospect as something they want. Focus on what's in it for them, stress the benefits and make them feel like it is something they absolutely must have, that it is something they wouldn't want to live without.

People also buy because they get pleasure from what they buy. Someone doesn't walk into a car dealership and buy a top of the line Mercedes because they need it; a nice Toyota or Chevy would have done the job just as well.

They buy the Mercedes because they want that feeling of pleasure that they feel every time they drive it. Whether it is the comfort of the plush leather seats, all the shiny gadgets, or the fact that it is a status symbol, they just love driving their Mercedes!

Whatever their reasons for buying that Mercedes, you can rest assured that their decision was based on want and not need.

Want is not the only thing that motivates people to make a purchase. While it is the leading contender, there are many other triggers that will motivate them to whip out their wallets and buy your product or service. There are a few basic categories of triggers including:

- **Problem:** your product can help solve their troubles and alleviate their pain

- **Greed:** it can help them gain more of something (like money)

- **Fear:** it can make them feel secure from threats, diseases, or general risks

- **Satisfaction:** it fulfills their want for enjoyment
- **Vanity:** it makes them look good or feel great
- **Trend:** they buy because everybody else owns it

More specifically, it's easier to trigger a purchase if you can show them some "hows", like how to:

- make more money
- save time
- be more comfortable
- be healthier
- be popular
- increase enjoyment
- attract the opposite sex
- have better sex
- escape pain and sadness
- avoid trouble
- make life easier
- take advantage of opportunities

These are only a few of the triggers that will motivate people to buy, but all triggers (ok, most triggers) fall into the categories listed earlier. If you want to learn how to effectively motivate your prospects to take action, then you need to find out what they want and then present your product or service to them in a manner that makes them feel like they can't live without it.

Hey if you can meet their needs at the same time—even better.

BONUS – REFERRALS

So you've taken in the 12 chapters of great information and thought provokers, but wait! This guide has a bonus just for you.

Referrals are important especially if you want to keep the sales coming and increasing. Referrals are a cost effective way to grow your business.

So how can one get referrals?

Search the Internet and you will be bombarded with a lot of sites and blogs that claim to give you the best way to get referrals. I have listed a few recommended options in this chapter:

Be referable

You should ensure that you deliver what you promise. Have a healthy relationship with your clients. Be sincere about what you're selling. With this, there is a possibility that you and your product or service will be referred by your satisfied customers. Yet take note, relying on this isn't enough to keep the referrals coming. Nevertheless, you will never get a referral if you are not referable.

Join professional organizations or associations

Some known groups are Le Tip, BNI and Toastmasters International. These are organizations comprised by intelligent, like-minded professionals that are immersed in the inner workings of the entrepreneurial mind-set to gather and provide participants with access to a variety of opinions and ideas. Groups have their assemblies wherein you get to mingle with other members, establish friendships, grow your professional skill set, and share referrals.

Ask for referrals

The best way to get referrals is to ask them from happy customers. Many salespeople have a fear of asking for referrals. Remember, people are glad to help others if it doesn't cost them anything (in dollars or credibility). You can start by saying that you're happy that they're pleased and could give them a few extra business cards. In that way, it would be easier for them to pass on your contact information.

Encourage virtual referrals.

Earlier, we discussed auto responders and how they automatically send customized e-mails to your mailing list. Speaking of this, add a tagline on the e-mail for those who have bought your product or service which says "Your recommendations and referrals are greatly appreciated" or to make it easier for them to add social buttons that say, "Love our service? Share it with your friends on twitter, e-mail or etc."

There are a lot of cost-efficient ways to gain referrals. All you need to do is to perform at your peak and make sure that your product or service does what it is supposed to do. Always remember that the best referrals will come from happy customers.

CONCLUSION

Now that you know the 12 Simple Steps to Better Sales [and additional ideas to help grow your business and increase your sales], we hope that you are primed and eager to test your renewed knowledge out in the business world. Competition may be fierce, but every challenge that comes your way is also an opportunity to learn and improve. Don't worry if you're not an expert yet. Return to this guide for a refresher whenever you need it. Each encounter in your business is a learning experience that will help you grow towards success. These 12 steps, as simple as they are, will be useful whether you are just starting your business or branching out into a new areas, and we hope that they prove invaluable as your sales increases and your business grows larger and more successful.

ABOUT THE AUTHOR

Cassandra Fenyk is a dynamic marketer, speaker, and motivator with extensive experience in various B2B and B2C industries, and unlike many other website and social media consultants, she is also an established marketing professional with nearly 20 years of experience in developing and directing business-to-consumer and business-to-business market penetration strategies. She has spent the majority of her career entrenched in branding, messaging, strategic planning, and project management. She has a keen understanding of the selling process and the critical steps between the initial message, the final sale, and post-sale relationship maintenance. Combined with her knowledge and experience in managing social media and website SEO programs, these traits make her a great source of information and an invaluable resource for your business.

Most recently, Ms. Fenyk started her coaching business focusing on start-ups, small businesses, and entrepreneurs; and all the characteristics that entails. Shark Bite Coaching (www.sharkbitecoaching.com) is that business and if you would like more personalized assistance in avoiding common business pitfalls, overcoming obstacles to your business growth, and getting your business moving in the right direction, ask her and set up an appointment to discuss your ideas and goals.

RECOMMENDED READING LIST

The Tipping Point: How Little Things Can Make a Big Difference
Malcolm Gladwell

The Best Damn Sales Book Ever: 16 Rock-Solid Rules for Achieving Sales Success!
Warren Greshes

Influence: The Psychology of Persuasion
Robert B. Cialdini

Trust Me, I'm Lying: Confessions of a Media Manipulator
Ryan Holiday

To Sell is Human: The Surprising Truth About Moving Others
Daniel H. Pink

Jeffrey Gitomer's Little Red Book of Selling: 12.5 Principles of Sales Greatness: How to make sales FOREVER
Jeffrey Gitomer

LOOK FOR MORE BUSINESS-BUILDING AND BUSINESS EXCELLENCE BOOKS BY SHARK BITE COACHING ON AMAZON

Shark Bite Coaching
PO Box 373
Florham Park, NJ 07932
shark@sharkbitecoaching.com

A Note to the Reader:

This guide is intended to offer tips and guidance on increasing your sales through the incorporation of various methodologies pertaining to relationship building, etc. Consult your attorney, tax accountant, or other professional advisors before choosing the right path for you and your business.

www.sharkbitecoaching.com